Echoes

Or How I Heard the Sound

ADRIENNE CRAWFORD

authorHOUSE®

AuthorHouse™
1663 Liberty Drive
Bloomington, IN 47403
www.authorhouse.com
Phone: 1 (800) 839-8640

Published by AuthorHouse   06/01/2017

ISBN: 978-1-5246-9454-8 (sc)
ISBN: 978-1-5246-9453-1 (e)

Library of Congress Control Number: 2017908648

Print information available on the last page.

Dedication

This book is dedicated to women everywhere who know they are strong. And also to those who have yet to realize how truly strong they are. In particular, my two sisters, Alberta and Heather.

Alberta, next to me in age, full of faith. She expresses the fact that God is always for us.

Heather, my baby sister, there whenever I had a crisis in my life.

Somehow she always miraculously appeared.

Ecclesiastes 4:11 Again, if two lie down together, they will keep warm. But how can one be warm alone? Though one maybe overpowered by another, two can withstand him. And a threefold cord is not quickly broken.

Alberta, Heather and me, a threefold cord.

Whenever my sisters and I get together, we say the spirit of our Mom is there.

Her strength is present in us. And when we pray it is powerful.

Let me also mention my cousins, Sandra Lee and Khadijah. Growing up with them was a joy. Also Aunt Jessie, Aunt Tessie, Aunt Mary, Uncle Curtis, and Uncle James who loved and cared for us as their own.

Last but not least, my kids and grandkids, Malik, Tanya, and Maya, Kareem, Shameca, Khrista, Kara, Kadejra. Also Regina, Joshua, Solomon, and Elijah.

And last but not least my God and Savior Jesus Christ the only true and living God.

Acknowledgements

To all my friends at the Ladies Lifestyles, godly women who prayed with me about the book and allowed me to read my poems at our fellowship.

Friends and former coworkers also encouraged me and eagerly awaited this next book.

And my gym buddies who sweat it out with me on a weekly basis. It was actually at a Zumba class where I saw in the spirit I could and should do another book.

To all the ladies in my life from childhood until now who instilled in me a work ethic and encourage me as a woman to never quit and never stop believing you can fulfill your dreams.

My sister Heather Hesley who supplied the beautiful illustrations to the book.

The three s's, S S S standing for a Strong body, A Sound mind, and A Sure and Sensitive spirit. The physical body must be exercised to become strong as it is the vessel that carries our lives everyday. A mind needs to be sound to discern between truth and lies. And a sure and sensitive spirit, the inner man which ultimately rules the whole being.

And to Jesus, Lord and Savior, He has never let me down. He will rule forever and ever.

Meditations

Or the thoughts of my mind

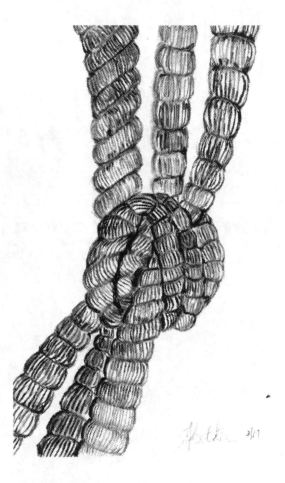

Rope of three cords

And so we begin.

Joel 2:28   Your old men shall dream dreams and your young men shall see visions......Visions.......we all need a vision of our future.....to see in the spirit where we are going or to see a new dream.......maybe one hid in our hearts, a new direction to go or a new plan you want to accomplish .... We must never let go of our dreams ... even though life sometimes sidetracks us with its daily demands ....dare to dream and get started on your vision. Peace

In your life you will come to a crossroads and you don't know what to do but you must choose......... Do something....it may not be the perfect right thing to do but do something.....if it is not right for you at least you will know what not to do ....next time.

Some things ....life.....you are always going to go through some things...as soon as you finish going through this thing a new thing will appear .. So here we are again with some things to go through... the only question is how are you going through the some things and do these things make you better or worse.....stronger or weaker? SOME THINGS, LIFE

Love ..it never hurts to love someone ...love expands our hearts even if you are not loved in return.......you loving helps you ... it makes you brand new ...so never fail to love someone more for your sake than theirs.....Love

Walking ....such a simple thing ...something we do every day ...we take it for granted yet such a profound thing.....whenever we need to make a change in our life ...it begins with taking a step, one at a time... simple ... yet for some so hard to do, start, with one small step ... BEGIN, ... ONE STEP AT A TIME ...TURN TO YOUR DESTINY... WALK ....STEP

1

They say life is short but actually life is long......you should plan for the future but live each day to the max.....be present in your life....which is but a breath and our minds are so fragile ..one wrong turn and our whole world can change ..be in the here and now..... Love God and love yourself and only then you can truly love others.

Progress.....we take two steps forward and one back but we are still moving forward..... we are making progress even though we may not feel as though we are ... at this point we may want to jump ship,,, but persevere...you will get there if you don't quit.

Life ... in life we're all on a journey...sometimes we get so focused on the goal whether it I raising kids, working, trying to get a degree....sometimes we lose sight that it is a journey and we have to enjoy just the trip...and the moments in between... we have to laugh at our mistakes and all the silly things we did in our youth AND our old age and be thankful we're still alive ..... we made it this far so don't stress, we'll make it the rest of the way...how you say?..... Somehow... the way we always made it....so stop and smell the roses ..or the coffee if you prefer...life is too short...laugh all you can...because if you think about it every little thing is funny.

To all the women and girls and anyone else out there who had no father ...or did not have a good relationship with their father, maybe he was absent or maybe he just could not be there for you in the way you needed him to be.....we must remember our fathers maybe didn't have a good relationship with their fathers ... so they can only give what they received ...we have to forgive them for our own sake ... because God is my father I was able through Him to forgive my own father and and not remember any hurt I felt for his absence....God is the only father I needed and all the father you need.....Bless His Holy name forever.

Intuition... what is the feeling you get that tells you when something is right or wrong......where does that information come from? It is the intelligence inside that is always on......that reads all things...that let's you know when something is not quite right.....it is the accumulation of all the info you are collecting at all times without even realizing it......

sometimes we meet someone or are in a situation and we feel a certain way and our conscious minds want to dismiss our first thought but I find the first thought is usually the best thought of what is really going on. So I'm learning to trust that first thought because I'm finding more and more it is the correct appraisal of what is actually happening.

Things happen..... Some of them bad or they seem bad but let us examine them...is it possible for you to see the bad things that happen to you as good things because you can use them to propel you to the things you really want? ... can we learn that these things that we go through are to teach us how to achieve our dreams?

Live your life, love your life, laugh at your life........lighten up, it will all be alright.

Be strong in yourself.

Be strong enough to be yourself. Be strong enough to not be swayed by the opinions and values that anyone places on you. You are you. Totally unique in all the world. You are wonderfully and fearfully made by a Creator who totally loves and supports you. Know yourself, you can be alone and not be lonely.

Take the time to get to know your own uniqueness.

The Birthright and The Blessing Gen.25 29 to 34 Esau sold his birthright, his rights as the first born son to his brother Jacob for a bowl of stew. Not having regard for what that meant.

Gen. 27 1 to 29 Then Jacob stole the blessing of his father Isaac by posing as his brother. The blessing was meant for Esau.

Think about the birthright, certain rights, privileges that belong to the firstborn. The blessing, the legacy handed down through a family line.

What is your birthright? What place in your family has responsibilities you must fulfill.

And the blessing ---the legacy--. Do your receive it and try to fulfill your role?

Mistakes...... we are not our mistakes...nor are we defined by the mistakes we made. We can learn from them and let them go. That which was done yesterday is past. Only today exists...only now. Being human we will fail and sometimes we dwell on the negative things we have done thereby robbing us of the present. Is it worth the gift of time you have been given today? Time that will never be replaced. Is it truly worth it?

Flexibility.....sometimes we hear our bones creak as we get up or move about, particularly as we age. We need to stretch our muscles to keep them limber. The same is true of our minds and lives. Flexibility or being able to yield at times when yielding is needed. When tough times come we can't be so set on one way yo do things but be open to other ideas and ways of doing things. Be flexible...you'll live longer.

1 King's 17 3 to 7   Are you by the brook barely eating bread and meat dropped by a raven's mouth and drinking water from a brook about to dry up? .....by the brook is a place in your life God is providing but it looks like the provision is about to run out. ...It did and then the Lord commanded Elijah to go to a little widow to get his provision ... it seems improbable but the Lord knows what He is doing...sometimes His directives don't make any sense to our natural minds ... if we will only obey....provision will be there.... by the brook..... Or by the little widow...

Matt. 8 23 to 27   Jesus asleep in the boat, the storm raging all around the disciples....what storm is raging in your life? Is Jesus with you in the boat?.... Then don't fear, the storm can't hurt you....Jesus was so unafraid He was asleep. ....how calm is that!!!!!!!!!!! Jesus knew nothing could hurt Him as he had to fulfill His destiny...so we will fulfill our destiny. Whatever storm is raging know this if you will remain calm God will deliver you from the storm ....have peace in the middle of your storm...... Peace

I find we get so stressed in our minds worrying about everything ... so many things we can't control and when we are in this state our mind we can't find the solutions to whatever we perceive our problems to be......in a relaxed state of mind we can think....the solution is always right next to the problem, we mainly can't see it ....but when we relax and realize there always is an answer ...it may be apparent right away or may come after some time has passed..... first we must realize that there always is a solution...let your mind be at rest and the answer will come... Know That

What will a new year bring?.....new things, some good maybe some not so good .. Yet we will live through it all...our job is to have joy regardless of what comes.....feel your joy, feel your peace, feel life...life is good because we are alive...live really live each day and be happy... find things to be happy about... I do...it makes me feel good ... how about you?

Man, the love for a woman by a man......each person wants to share his own true self ..the self we keep hidden from the world hoping that someone somewhere will love the us as we truly are ... we have the tendency to love those who are who we want them to be or to love them when they do what we want them to do......rather then loving them for themselves, ... we only want to see them reflected in our eyes, once they deviate from that we no longer revere them... thank goodness God does not love the way we humans do or He would have disregarded us a long time ago.

Whatever is bothering you I ask the question will it be bothering you in 5 years from now? ...how about 10 years from now? No ...you'll only laugh about it then......well you might as well shorten the time frame.. laugh about it now and save yourself some worry.

The caterpillar......think of an ugly creature crawling on the ground who decides to go into the leaf....hidden from view and after a time emerges as a beautiful butterfly..........a miracle, yes he is the same as us ... some times we think of ourselves as an ugly creature crawling around or others may make us feel this way, yet inside of each of us is a beautiful butterfly waiting to come out and fly.....It's all in there ...let your butterfly free.

Thinking usually your first thought is your most correct assessment of any situation. ...your gut is telling you the truth of any matter facing you.... check it out..... see if your first impression is the right one.

Do you realize who you really are .. The fact that you walk and talk and live should tell you that you are a powerful being ....made in the image of God ...your creator who created you to be a creator like Himself and you have a great deal of say in the way you live your life. Are you joyful and thankful for all your experiences good and bad?... meant to teach us and grow us up to our full potential. Cherish every tear and wrest the benefit out of it.....use the lesson to make your future better and brighter.

Butterfly....more thoughts ... I wondered where I was in my butterfly path... was I still a caterpillar just starting to enter the leaf or just emerging wings still wet? perhaps already beginning to take my first flight, wings aching to fly high in the sky just testing them out to see if I can really soar. Who knows? We are all at different stages in our growth and knowledge... today examine yourself and see if your wings are dry so your flight can take you where you want to go.

Breathe ...just breathe....sometimes you need to just breathe....let it out..... whatever you are going through it will pass...just relax and breathe....in the end you will be glad you let whatever is holding you back go......JUST BREATHE

All you have to do in life is figure out the next right move and do it.

Female eyes

Forgotten

Moses, on the backside of a mountain. For 40 years he waited. He knew he was the deliverer but through a hasty, bad decision he set back his own destiny. 40 years of waiting for God to call him to his right place.

How many of us would have long forgot our calling yet when he saw a bush that was burning but not consumed he stepped into his future. 40 years, a long time to wait. Yet God is never too early or too late. 40 years. Could you or I wait that long? 40 years.

Sometimes.......We think we have such a hard life. Yet look at the Apostle Paul. How much he suffered for the cross of Christ. He preached and taught and was yet was imprisoned. And to think he wrote so much of the New Testament from a jail cell. Telling us things such as, Rejoice again I say rejoice. From a prison. Are you rejoicing from what ever you perceive to be a jail cell in your life?

True Power

We hold the power of our experience. We're not always able to control our circumstances but we have a great deal to say in how we react to what happens to us. Our power comes from the choices we make every day, minute by minute. When we find our real selves hiding during any circumstance and are able to connect to that, then that ability is our true power. Our job is to search out ways to come to the knowledge of our true selves.

Prickly.......Someone who gets under your skin. They just seem to rub you the wrong way, like sandpaper. Yet you have to deal with them. No escape. Think this way, maybe they're in your life...like that sandpaper, to rub some of the rough edges off of you. Make you more patient. So relax, let them rub and one day you'll be a polished precious gem.

Numbers 12 1 to 16

Miriam and Aaron spoke against Moses because he married an Ethiopian woman. Haters .....So they rebelled against God's anointed man Moses. Sometimes people become bitter because of things happening in their lives. So they get a very hard spirit in them, become jealous and have a harsh judgement of others.

But that is not a good thing. We don't know what God is doing in someone else's life. And bitterness never destroys another, it destroys you.

Protocol....... A code of diplomatic or military rules of behavior...my thoughts, Joseph learned protocol when he was in prison and serving the 2 officers of pharaoh... he learned all about how pharaoh's court was run as he served them ... and he even knew to shave because all Egyptian's hate beards...so he took advantage of where he was at and learned all he could ... so that when God raised him to be second in command he knew how to do... Protocol

Stillness .... silence... I find in the world we live in a need for time alone... so much info is thrown at us on a daily basis that it becomes necessary to obtain some inner peace to deal with all of it..... We need a place and time, usually daily where we can just download all of the things we take in...no cellphone, no tv, no videos, no contact with others ... just you....meditate .....be still and listen to your own heart...quiet your mind... commune with God ...let go of today's events or just sit and do nothing...... it's good if you can do it outside ..but have a quiet place for you and you alone .... I think you will be refreshed.

Gen 15 1 to 6   God had promised Abram that his offspring would inherit the land of Canaan but he had no children and his body was old... God said, "Look at the stars of heaven and count them if you are able to number them..so shall your descendants be".... In other words don't look at your own body weakness or the fact that you have no children. So we shouldn't look at our present circumstances or any weakness in our physical body... look to God who is greater than all and we His children are promised His provision... so what are you looking at?

A question.....have you ever seen a bird siting on the curb with his head in his hands wondering how he as going to feed his little birdies? NO... a bird knows there is some food out here some where so he goes searching for it... we are more valuable to God than a bird ...yet we worry...actually worry is an insult to God,..it is over concern about tomorrow which we don't have control over anyway. God made the birds and us too... if we are His children and we are, why do we worry?....take a lesson from the birds.... don't worry about anything... trust God ... everything is going to be alright.

Habits ... things you do everyday without thinking .... good habits save you time and energy... bad habits... not so good sometimes we do things thinking we can control them but somehow they end up controlling us... habits ... what are yours?

Jesus said with God all things are possible.......such an encouraging word . ...ALL THINGS ARE POSSIBLE...........ALL THINGS ARE POSSIBLE ....ALL THINGS ARE POSSIBLE......I'm saying it a lot over in my mind to make myself realize All things are possible......what are we afraid of? God said with me All things are possible.... Believe it and receive it ......ALL THINGS ARE POSSIBLE.

Did you make a mistake? ...go down the wrong path? ... turn left when you should have turned right? Well don't worry you can begin again. .... It is only a loss if you didn't learn something from it. Use it as a stepping stone of knowledge to make the right decision and one thing you know not to do again.

Some people see the glass as half empty or half full. I see it as full and running over, so full that even though it is emptying it is being replenished at the same time ie the more you give out the more your cup is refilled...... Hallelujah

The past ... the thing about the past is that it is past, meaning it's over.... let it go especially if it is a bad memory....don't relive it as it is gone..... Live fully now cause all we ever have is now.... Which is ever new and you can make it be anything you want it to be.....only you have the power to make your now be like wow.

Sometimes we over think things, we tie ourselves in knots trying to think our way through things, it gets us nowhere expect tied into more knots... we need to let go and feel.... Rest and know the answer is coming ... realize good is on the way...let go and trust God,.... let go, stop thinking so much feel, relax and rest.

Get to know your true inner self...be all the way present in your life...show up..be who you were truly meant to be....... be you ......

Swag .... let's talk about it ..you gotta have swag to deal to with the issues in your life....an attitude that says whatever happens to me I WILL BE VICTORIOUS ..I will never quit, never give up and the fact that I am a child of the Most High God... the One who rules and reigns in the heavens ... the One who looks down on earth and laughs at fools who try to come against Him and His Anointed.

There are different kinds of smart people ....more than I can enumerate here.....1.. A smart person ..just naturally smart..... 2.. book smart... able to learn from books....3..slick. A little underhanded... 4...quick...able to discern a situation very fast...5 street smart....wise in the ways of the street... book smart ..an example of Benjamin Franklin ... a man could say horse in 9 languages.... .but bought a cow to ride on....how many ways are you smart?......and how can you learn to get smart in the ways you are not?

Conversely....Talking about people who are not so smart we say....not playing with a full deck....the elevator doesn't go up to the top floor....their bread isn't baked.....lost their marbles or they have a bag full of marbles but the bag has a hole in it...and last but not least ....his cheese slid off the cracker.

1 Samuel 30:6 Now David was greatly distressed, for the people spoke of stoning him, because the soul of all the people was grieved, every man for his sons and daughters... But David strengthened himself in the Lord..... I imagine he left them and got into a quiet place and he remembered how God had delivered him many times. When he was alone with the sheep forgotten by his dad and his brothers. Yet God protected him when he fought the bear and lion trying to eat the lambs. So he remembered and knew for certain that the God who had delivered him many times would deliver him again from the people's wrath.... God our deliverer and the One who strengthens us.... Always remember and

Never forget His hand on your life.

The law of God..Jesus said love God with all your heart and love your neighbor as yourself. Most times we love God as well as we can. Where we usually get tripped up at is in loving our neighbor as ourselves mainly because we don't love ourselves first. We don't realize we are many people inside ie we have different aspects of our personality existing in our one body. We were a child and a young adult now grown, where did the child go? Or the young adult? The aspects of that person is still inside. But we are older now and yet we still don't know our full potential. We limit ourselves and get caught up in our daily lives...and we wonder why we are so dissatisfied. We need time to process where we are and what we are doing. Do we have dreams unfulfilled? Are we following our hearts? What desires are we still longing to pursue? Do we realize in our lifetime we will sometimes be single, sometimes in school and sometimes busy with raising a family. Yet life is an ongoing learning experience. Where are we and how we can know ourselves better and become who we truly want to be.

Female lips

Hard

Hard .... The hardest thing in the world to do, start ..... A new diet ... an exercise plan....any change to make yourself better......but we need to just begin and...... begin right now.....

2nd hardest thing you'll ever do... fail at something, fall off the wagon, relapse .....is to forgive yourself, get back up, start again, and move forward......get back on the horse!!!!!!!!!!!!!!!! A child when he is learning to walk will fall over and over again until he learns how to walk...and he doesn't berate himself for falling down....so start.

There was a commercial on TV about a spaghetti sauce.....it said it's all in there ..it was talking about the ingredients .. we humans are like that.... whatever we need it's all in us ...most times we don't know what is in us. God as creator put everything we need there, what's going on inside us determines what is happening in our outer life....change your inner life, what are you thinking about? ... we don't know our own strength ...we feel tired so we don't exercise not realizing exercise gives us energy... our bodies are amazing machines that have the capacity to do great things... it's all in there.....use it

Bad habits.... Overeating, trying to fill some hole that food can never fill. Then we get angry at ourselves for overeating which makes us more depressed so we eat more...or our minds are filled with past memories of failures going forward ..if you hurt someone make amends if you can...... if someone has hurt you forgive them for your own sake....if you've done wrong forgive yourself and change your ways.

Sometimes someone is trying to tell you something but you can't hear because of the package it comes in as how the person looks or the way they are dressed.....A 15 year old thinks what his parents are saying is ridiculous, then when he turns 25 suddenly his parents are brilliant....did his parents change? No the child grew up.....

Matt..13 54 to 57 Jesus when He had come to His own country He taught them in their synagogue so that they were astonished and said "Where did this man get this wisdom and these mighty works? Is it not the carpenter's son? Is not His mother Mary? And His brothers James, Joses, Simon and Judas and His sisters are they not all with us?... Where did this man get all these things? So they were offended at Him...but Jesus said to them "A prophet is not without honor except in his own country and in his own house"....so be careful how you hear......be careful what you hear and don't dismiss the message because of the way the messenger looks.

I only say one thing all day [or at least I try to] I enjoy ...I enjoy everything ... the good and the bad ...I experience life in the now....because now is all there is .....I enjoy everything.......think about it, God gave us a way to replenish our batteries to live 3 times a day with something that refreshes, eating and the more healthy we eat the better we feel...I enjoy people all shapes and sizes wouldn't it boring if we all were the same ...I enjoy exercising as it strengthens the body....I enjoy laughter as it cleanses the soul and I laugh at myself, my mistakes and past disappointments knowing I was doing the best I knew how at the time..... .so I forgive myself and love myself because it took all those things to make me who I am today... hopefully wiser and happier with who I really am.....

Looking back ... in doing that we hold on to what was.....our inability to accept loss can keep us from moving forward....its like driving while looking in the rearview mirror ... sooner or later you're gonna have a crash ... when you hold on to what you had there is no way to create and see your future...so where do we go from here?.... Remember Lot's wife .... she had to look back....

Judges 6 12 to 14   And the Angel of the Lord appeared to him [Gideon] and said to him, "The Lord is With you, you mighty man of valor" then the Lord turned to him and said "Go in this might of yours and you shall save Israel from the hand of the Midianites, have I not sent you?" so he said to Him "O my Lord, How can I save Israel? Indeed my clan is the weakest in Manasseh and I am the least in my father's house." Gideon didn't see himself as God did. Sometimes we don't see ourselves as God sees us. Gideon felt weak and ineffectual but God knew what He had put in Gideon. So we have to realize there is more to us than meets the eye.

What a wonderful thing is the beginning of a new day....to think it starts every morning .. A new chance to start over, to rejoice in God, to love your family, to renew old friendships, to forgive our enemies, the possibilities are endless. Thank you Lord for this precious gift of TODAY

Let's talk about recognition Exodus 1:11 and onward. When Moses killed the Egyptian and the next day he assumed his brethren would recognize him as their deliverer... he was shocked to find out they didn't acknowledge him as such..........when Moses went before Pharaoh, the king he didn't recognize God, the I AM.....Pharaoh worshiped heathen gods made with a man's hand and since he was Pharaoh the greatest one on earth at that time, he no had no revelation of anyone greater than himself, he was pharaoh....so in our lives we must recognize who we are, where we are going and who God is ....in our lives... as the kids say RECOGNIZE!!!!!

Click ......click. That's the sound you hear when your life is coming together... when you're in the flow when everything is working right ... sort of like Dr. J flying up to the basket or Michael Jordan sailing through the air, how about Kobe scoring 81 points in a game....It's when the favor of God is on your life and great grace abounds toward you.... Click... Click... Click

The human condition when you get right down to it we are all creatures looking to connect to others as that is what we are created for... relationships... one heart calling out to another...our greatest joy is to connect to another on a deeper level... to be loved and accepted for who we really are with all our...flaws....knowing God accepts us as we are as He sees and knows us so intimately... why all the hairs on our head are numbered. So I say rejoice, One loves you so much and in an unconditional way...not as man does... rejoice, for you are much loved.

Babies ... A baby comes into the world knowing he is the center of the universe... when he's hungry or wet or uncomfortable he cries and when he is happy he coos or laughs and this can be 2 seconds apart...babies trust that someone will hear and take care of them...babies love themselves and are not bothered by your opinion of them... they don't worry about the future ... we should be more like babies... trust that God hears and will take care of us....love ourselves and don't let others bring us down.... stop worrying about the future ...and be free with our emotions... be quick to forgive and quick to laugh.........BABIES.

Each day is a gift...appreciate it ... the bad parts [which you'll get past] and the good parts which hopefully you can stretch out for longer and longer periods of times...laugh at all the good and the better you'll feel...gratitude makes for a better day, week, year and life.

People... the funny thing about people is you can never can change anyone but yourself. They are going to do what they are going to do ... the only thing you have control over is yourself ... so for peace in your life let them be... turn your attention to something good about them [even if you have to make it up] look or their positive side and you'll feel better which is really all we want anyway...to feel good and happy.

He Is

He is whatever you need Him for....He is.....Do you need a healer?....
He is.....Do you need a provider?.....He is....Do you need strength?......He
is.........Do you need peace?.....He is ....Do you need joy?.....He is.....He's an
ever present help in time of trouble.....HE IS...right now......HE IS.

I read somewhere ...prayer changes everything....mostly it changes you.

A story I read once. 2 frogs found themselves in a bucket of milk. One frog
said oh we'll never get out. I'm just going to lay here till I die. The other
frog said well the only thing I can do is swim around, I'm not going to lay
around till I die. So he swam and swam around in a circle. Eventually his
swimming caused the cream to be turned into butter which made a heap to
the top of the bucket from which he hopped out and saved his life. Never
give up and never give in to negative thinking. Keep on swimming!!!!

I heard this on a Joel Osteen sermon.....A man hitting a rock with a
hammer or whatever tool you would use. He kept hitting the rock, it
wouldn't split....but one day it split. What split the rock? Was it the 1st blow
no...was it the last blow..no it was all those blows in between.....it was the
day after day accumulation of blows that split it....perseverance.

Hebrews 11 1 & 3 Now faith is the substance of things hoped for the
evidence of things not seen. By faith we understand that worlds were made
by the word of God, so that the things which are seen were not made by
things which are visible.

Spiritual things are more powerful than physical things. Sometimes we are so busy looking at the physical thing {a problem that needs to be solved} we miss the fact that there is a spiritual force in us that is stronger than the physical problem. When we walk by faith the word and believe that we receive what we need and thank God for His provision before we see it it shall come to pass...The spirit is greater than the physical.

I read this somewhere.

3 Laws of money.....The 1st.... Never lose money........the 2nd ...never forget the 1st law.... And the 3rd is pay yourself first....save some money for you and your family before you pay anyone else.

John the Baptist, living in the wilderness with only one job, to announce to the world The One who was to come... He who was born in a manger, a babe yet a king worshipped by the magi...an infant yet who would one day save us from our sins..... One who was sheltered and taught by human parents but would one day confound the greatest minds of His day ...and John the Baptist living such a lonely life yet communing with God every day to carry out His purpose..... Jesus called him the greatest prophet...life sometimes so confusing and yet at times we have clear vision of who we are and what we are to do....what joy to know your purpose....Joy

Life is a journey, we are all on a path to find something that has everlasting value and meaning ... there will be hills and valleys on our path but there is One who travels with us ... we are never truly alone...although some people feel this aloneness, this separation from things and people ...yet the One who travels with us feels our pain and aloneness. He carries it in Himself if we will give it to Him...His shoulders are broader than ours and He is able to carry it...give Him all your pain and aloneness and let the load you carry for this journey be light.

Now. We are in the now ..now is.... now always is ... who I was yesterday is gone .. I am only who I am now.... now who I am is good ... it is a good feeling to be me now ...but tomorrow I will be better... my job is to realize no matter how I feel, good or bad ...that I must always get back to the joy of now.

Be easy, be easy in your life ..be easy on yourself .. ..be easy on others ... we are all searching for something ...be easy be light...be free, let others be themselves ... it's alright .. It's all good ... You be you and I'll be me ..it's alright ..it's all good ...be easy ...all things change in time ... change... whatever you are going through wait a little while ... it will change, so be easy.

Find a peaceful place to retreat when life's winds are buffering you..... whether that place is a physical place or just a rest in your mind ... the more you go there the more you'll be able to deal with the inevitable ups and downs of life....when you retreat there you get in touch with God who is always with you. He's always for you and He has all the answers ... sometimes the answer is to just rest and trust in Him as He has it all covered ... His mind is bigger than ours so He has the solution to our problem already...so relax ..the answer may not come from where you think it's going to come from but know the answer is coming ..and if you know the answer is coming you can relax and smile because the solution is on the way...actually the solution is already here...and if it is already here you might as well be happy right now!!!!

A leaning tree

Genesis 28 10 to 19

Jacob fleeing from his brother after his treachery. He came to a certain place and took a stone to lay down his head. He had a dream, a ladder going up to heaven with angels ascending and descending on it. He recognized he was in a Holy place and God was there. Sometimes in your life you will be somewhere where you will realize God is there and He is speaking to you.

It is a God moment. Where God actually interrupts your life to speak to you and give you a word in that season.

If you find yourself there, stop. Listen and go forward with a new clarity.

When you know who you are, you won't let others treat you the way they do. When you don't allow others to treat you in a disrespectful way, you will not be disrespected. You better know your worth.

The Acts 2:1 to 24   When the day of Pentecost had fully come a sound of a mighty rushing wind filled the room where the disciples were. And they all began to speak with new tongues and the room was in confusion. So Peter stood and addressed them. Peter who had denied Jesus three times and swore he never knew Him. Yet now commanding the room and expounding the scriptures. No longer afraid but bold. ..... That's what we need a spirit of boldness to not be afraid of life and to do what needs to be done and speak what needs to be said.

Be bold and unafraid!!!

See it!

Believe it!

Be it!

Trees,.......... if a tree has deep roots where it draws it's nourishment from far below the surface of the ground. You can be sure when the storms come that the tree will stand. It's foundation is steady and sure. We must have our roots grounded in a sure source, God, so when the adversity comes we'll stand. Rooted and grounded.

Your spirit....From the word of God we realize God breathed the breathe of life into man and we are primarily spirits. Our spirit is the life that is in us. Sometimes we feel so tired and depleted because we are speaking {breathing out} to people and giving our attention to those who do not reciprocate in kind. We give our energy to those who are not worthy, who demean us, who hide the true nature of their intentions toward us. Then we wonder why we feel the way we do. Maybe we can step back, examine the nature of the relationships we have and let go those that either don't lift us up or give us back the energy we have given them. We must have the courage to let them go. This is for our own peace of mind.

Genesis 37:18 to 28   In the pit. So Joseph was in the pit that his jealous brothers put him in and I'm sure he wondered was he ever going to get out. Sometimes we find ourselves in a low place where it seems there is no help for us. Yet the One who lives and rules and reigns knows exactly where we are. We are not alone and He has made a way of escape. Sometimes all we can do is trust in an unseen outcome. So do not give up hope, but only believe..... It will only last for a little while.

Responsibility...... I think the old have a responsibility to teach the young......we have been on earth a while and should have learned a thing or two about how to survive this long ... it is our obligation to pass on what we know to the next generation....I have wondered why I have been so stressed about so many things when everything turned out for the best so I am still learning to relax and go with the flow

Did you ever wonder why certain things happen to you or why you are in a certain place or why you know certain people? Just know God knows right where you are....He goes before us in a pillar of cloud by a day and a pillar of fire by night..... And He's already provided for you....in this natural realm we may not see where the money is coming but my God owns the cattle on a thousand sand hills and if we'll do all we know to do He will do the rest... God can chew gum and walk at the same time ..He is not hindered by anyone or anything ...If we'll thank Him for His provision before we see it will come to pass sometimes in unexpected ways...do a little dance in your living room ..praise Him in your car thank Him all day long....say the money will come, say My God supplies all my need.... expect God to do something good for you every day...we are His children and all dads want good for their children.... So believe it and receive it....... speak it and it shall come to pass.

Life is sometimes relatively simple .....whatever you don't feel like doing is probably the thing you probably should do....don't feel like going to work you go anyway ..don't feel like exercising exercise anyway.....don't feel like eating your veggies eat them anyway....don't feel like going to school.....go anyway...like Nike says just do it.

When you're older you're very conscious of your time ...as you wonder how much time is left to do something significant ... I discovered that it seems to take more time than you think to do anything.... Time ...one thing you can't get back again.

Acts. 26:1 to 2   I think myself happy, King Agrippa because today I shall answer for myself before you concerning all the things which I am accused by the Jews.....the apostle was Paul was a prisoner yet he thinks himself happy ....you are what you think ......think yourself happy and you will be....is the glass half full?

Ephesians 6:13 & 14

Therefore take up the whole armor of God that you may be able to withstand in the evil day and having done all, stand.

Stand therefore, having girded your waist with truth, having put on the breastplate of righteousness.

Stand..........Stand when you are going thru something and you feel like fainting...

Stand ... when enemies come against you ....Stand .....when your money ain't right and it looks like you are not going to make it.....

Stand.

Dreams

Do you dare to dream again? Yesterday is dead and gone, yet what you dreamed about in your past may still be able to come to pass. What skills and talents lay buried inside? Did life get in your way as it has a habit of doing?

Yet there is a vague unease somewhere deep inside? Maybe you can take one step toward your life's passion. That one thing you could do all day without getting tired. It's not even work to you but pure joy. All it takes is one step... ONE

Do you have a friend who is like a touchstone? One you've known for years that lets you know just where you are. They are a mirror to give you a reflection of yourself. That helps you to stay on your path or get back on the road if you've wandered off. A touchstone, every one needs one.

It takes courage to be unique.

Validation......Do you find you seek the approval of others for how you live your life? Is it necessary that you fit into their little circle? Maybe you haven't learned exactly who it is you are. Even if you try to make someone else happy by being what you perceive they want you to be. You will never attain that. People are always changing and so are you. No person outside yourself can tell you who you really are........So you might as well be yourself and make yourself happy. At least one of you is feeling good.

Body, Soul and Spirit......the three areas of life...in each we need balance. To have a strong body some form of exercise is needed and good nutritious food, to not overeat.......the soul or mind needs soundness, clarity and wholesome things to think about...we have some much power in our thoughts to change the course of our lives and spiritual... who or what principles guide your life?

Do you have a belief in a higher power outside yourself or do you just go by your own intellect? It makes a difference what you believe in, how the course of your life flows... somethings to think about.

Lady smelling a flower

Saxifrage

Saxifrage.... The flower that splits the rock. Sometimes in life you find yourself in a hard place. Maybe you are married to a man who doesn't quite understand you which causes you grief. Yet you know you must stay with him. And somehow you grow thru a difficult situation.

Whereas you really would think a strong rock would crush a flower. Yet the flower grows in a crack in the rock and splits it.

Such strength found in such a small thing. Never discount your ability to flourish even though where you are looks like an impossible place.

It is now the time to tell yourself that no one can validate you. What you feel, what you know, what you can do or how God is manifesting His life and gifts in you and thru you. Your gift is yours. Naturally you need constructive criticism but others who speak negatively about you and who you truly are need to be let go. Just let these folks go.

Every coat doesn't fit everybody.

1 Samuel 17:39

David ready to face Goliath. He fastened his sword to his armor and tried to walk and couldn't. So he said to Saul, I cannot walk with these for I have not tested them. Meaning he wasn't used to fighting with armor on.

Sometimes we try to fit into another man's coat. We admire him and maybe want to be like him. Yet if we tried on his coat it would not fit. We need our own coat, one that fits us. So we can move the way we want to.

Joseph and his coats.... Think about it... His father gave him a coat of many colors as he was beloved by Jacob. You know the story. Then later on when he was sold into slavery by his brothers to Potiphar and Potiphar's wife sought to lay with him he fled as she grabbed his coat. She used this garment to accuse Joseph who was then put into prison. Many years he languished there until Pharaoh had a dream which Joseph interpreted. Pharaoh raised him up to be the second in command. Naturally Pharaoh gave garments of linen, his own signet ring and a gold chain around his neck.

Three different coats... three different times in his life.... Three separate circumstances.... The first coat, God gave him a vision of his future. The second coat he was accused of wrong he did not do. But oh the third coat, he was lifted up and ruled the land of Egypt second only to Pharaoh.

God always knows what He is doing, trust Him thru all your trials and tribulations. He will reward those who follow Him.

2 Corinthians 12:7

The thorn in the flesh. Sent to harass us and cause us grief. Anything major in our makeup which buffets us continuously. God has allowed it so that His power is made available to us in our weakness. To help us remember we must depend on Him.

He does not remove it but gives us grace to bear it.

Great grace is needed.

The place of meeting......where God comes down to meets us. A God moment in our life where heaven and earth meet. There the ground is holy and we sense God's presence. He's come to speak to us a word. To give us direction for our life.

Exercise.....a funny thing about exercise. It seems like exercise would make you more tired but actually it gives you more energy. An object that is in motion tends to stay in motion. A person that keeps sitting finds it hard to get moving. So start out slowly but at least get started.

Waiting on God.......Sometimes we are waiting for God to move in our lives. Yet He is telling us he's waiting for us to move. He will move and is just letting us know He is already with us and we have all we need. We must go forward with what we know to do. It is a marvel to me that God needs us to move, but He does. We are His hands and heart in the earth. So move we should and He will back us up.

Passion ...it is the enthusiasm in our lives. The joy in our hearts when we get up in the morning looking ahead to a glorious day. It gives us the energy to do what it is we love the most and can do all day and never get tired. To be able to pursue our talents with ease. Learn what is your passion and seek to do it with all your might.

Sometimes we listen to so many other voices. The ones in our lives and voices from the past that tell us we can't do or become what we need to be. We may have dreams and visions of our future that seem to us to be impossible. But God is no respecter of persons. If He placed a dream there know for sure it can be accomplished.

There are days when I realize I'm not where I need to be. The hopes I had for my life were sometimes deferred by myself and I listened to voices that I thought knew more than me. They discouraged me from my path because they didn't see me as I really was. That was my fault for not recognizing that I am the only one who has the key to me. It took years to begin to say to myself that I am alright just the way I am. Having gone thru certain things gave me strength and a revelation of myself. To becoming mature enough to be able to say no the those voices and hear my own. The truest measure of me.

Listen to the wind, it talks.

Listen to the silence, it speaks.

Listen to your heart, it knows.

Musings

Or the poems of my heart

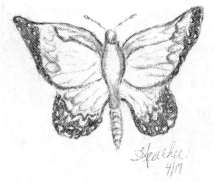

Two Women
Two Butterflies

Two Women

Two women
Troopers and friends
Trudging thru the airports of their lives.
Alive they are
As they fade to black,
And answer each other's questions
Before the words
Escaped from lips,
Painted red.
With a new shade of lipstick.
A pick me up
For a life alone.
Friends for just about
Ever- never to be
Severed by any man
Or test of time.
Divine they are together
Managing to weather all
Storms and thunder showers.
No matter how strong
The winds blow.
Two girls who know
And love each other
As themselves
No longer 2 selves but one
Proceeding to their
Separate destinies,
Free, you see.

I Always Knew

I always knew
Who I was becoming.
I always knew the day
When I would stop running.
From the person I was
To whom I'm meant to be.
From the little girl
To the woman now I see.
I cut my hair off short.
I look like Momma now.
But that is all ok.
My Mom was such a wow
Person in my life,
Strong as can be.
With a heart so big.
It makes me happy
To be identified
With a woman of her degree.
And to be her daughter
Her face in my mirror I see.
Having a clear mind
And a body so sturdy.
With a spirit so focused
On what I want to be.
So I progress
To where love exists,
Knowing I can never rest
But be always in the mix.
And do what needs to be
Done, to journey on.
Showing all the world
How I sing my song.

The Road Called Tired

The road called tired.
A place I used to know.
Has come back to visit.
And to put on it's show.
I'm living from a place named wiped.
As in out, you get the drift.
Like a credit card when it's swiped.
Or a beating when you get kicked.
I've settled in a town called beat.
And I really need to lay down.
And, put up my feet.
And allow my mind to frown.
I'm a biding in a quiet space.
Where no one else is around.
I'm waiting for the night.
When I can't hear any sound.
I'm residing in a special area.
Where no aliens are found.
But maybe they'll send a spaceship.
Taking me to the moon so round.
There I'll be able to rest.
And catch up on my sleep.
There I can lay down.
And nap with nary a peep.
Then I'll be very able
To get the repose I need
I'll pull up the blankets
Covering my toes to my knees.

Surrender

When you surrender
To all that is.
When you give up
Your own way to live.
To be open
To God's plan.
To rest in Him
And to understand.
Your life is on
A path you see.
Where you're walking
Is where you'll be.
And where you are
Is where you can't flee.
Your steps are ordered
Tread lightly and free.
Seek the direction
How your life can agree.
Realize time will
Be all you need.
You find what you love.
Your joy breaks free.
Of chains and shackles
Becoming an escapee.
Then mountains will disappear
Into the sea.
As you pray for solutions
On bended knee.
Look at the clouds
And the bumblebee.
Each one yearning
To fill it's destiny.
And your journey

Will have a marquee.
A flashing sign
And to a high degree.
Others will recognize
You are so carefree.
Cause you uncovered
An important discovery.
You've found a road
You've found a key.
To living your life
With no apology.
Living your days
Not as an absentee.
But loving your moments
As an attendee,
In your own walk
As a devotee,
Of all that is good
And full of fantasy,
Of your present reality.
You'll end your days
Filled with glee.
And peace to have found
Your own jubilee.

My Life Is Set to Music

My life is set to music.
All of life a song.
I hear it all the time.
Music's where I belong.
The clefs and notes I hear.
As I live my life.
Are just the melodies.
With which my life is rife.
I sing my song all day.
And when you see me smile.
It's because I'm happy.
And joyful all the while.
My days have twists and turns.
And false starts that I do.
I know that in the end,
I will become brand new.
I love to listen to
A sound played so clear.
That it reverberates
Into my waiting ear.
Loving to hear how.
The words come together,
With the music in a tune.
And how they seem whether
It's sung or it's crooned.
And so the life I lead.
Has a distinct sound.
So open up and heed.
You'll find it so profound.
And then you can attune.
Your ears to your own voice,
When you sing your song
You'll know you have a choice

Of where your hours will go.
And what you want to do,
Where you'll feel your flow.
The song you sing so true.
In your very heart.
Will be the one you live.
The one that will start.
You on your way to give
You fame, fortune if you choose.
Your song will be the one.
In which you cannot lose.
It will be your number one.
The only piece you need.
It will be the very best.
This you must believe.

Planets and Cosmos

On The Day I was Born

On the day I was born.
Many things were happening.
The sun shone bright that morn.
And stars began to sing.
Supernovas totally exploded.
And galaxies were flung in space.
Moons orbited their planets.
And comets started to race.
The planets all aligned.
And the moon put on his face.
Black holes suddenly had light.
And constellations fell in place.
Cosmic events were held that day.
And meteors traveled to earth.
Total eclipses had their say.
It was because I had worth.
And also so do you.
Being born can you remember?
What the heavens commenced to do.
Whether it was June or September.
It was special day too.
When you came into the world.
Angels had a clue.
That a unique boy or girl.
Had entered the atmosphere.
Sent from God above.
To live in this hemisphere.
And to share all His love.

Let's Jump Back Into Plank

Let's jump back into plank.
No, I'll just stay put.
When you finish that move
Then I'll move onto my foot.
Let's jump back into plank.
Lift your left leg up and thank,
Your lucky stars you can,
Do a great head stand.
But I say to you.
My legs don't want to do.
A head stand or a plank
And it's you I have to thank,
For all these limber joints.
You get right to the point.
Do a chaturanga good.
And know your legs should
Do warrior one well.
Downward dog can always tell,
If your yoga practice is working.
It's so much better than twerking.
And child's pose always let's.
Us get a little rest.
From these varied stances.
Much slower than most dances.
Making us freeze
For a time.
On our knees
They help us unwind.
Thank you, for being so kind.

The Condition

What is the condition of your condition?
Are we living in the fiction
We will never die?
We try and push back time
With gym visits and vitamins.
Can we win?
Will the grim reaper
Sleep a little bit longer?
And pass us by as we attempt
To cheat him of his hour.
Will the shower and shadow of death
Help us live for the now?
Can we somehow ignore this knowledge
And attempt to be exempt from
His scythe?
So with, that thought in mind.
Keep going to the gym.
Keep loving the him,
Or her in your life.
Keep teaching the grands.
Keep in touch with old friends.
Keep on keeping on
Til our song
Is no more.
We'll close the door.
They'll know we endured.
And our love for them was sure.

In The Sunset Of My Years

In the sunset of my years
I tramp thru roads
And see other's tears,
Falling quickly.
And I press forward
To a new age
As a new sage.
Unafraid to speak my mind.
Sometimes not very kind
To younger folks
Who choke on
The vowels coming straight from a heart.
True sounds
That abound and
Tell you to be aware.
Share
And do care
For others.
I smother back
Advice I should dispense.
But fences put up by those
Who dispose of their brains
In time of need.
They don't heed the
Warning signs of
Do not taste,
Do not touch,
Do not hear.
But being the seer
I am.
I see in the future.
The suture that will
Bind the wounds

Of others mistakes.
My take on life is deep
As I repeat
Phrases my momma said
Wisdom from one
Now dead
But still speaking.
So I repeat,
I repeat.

The Mystery Of The Moment.

The mystery of the moment.
The secret of the hour.
The consensus of a day.
That time has the power.
The lifting of a window.
The opening of a door.
The separateness of humans.
Sometimes from one adored.
The loneliness of living.
All of us feel the pain.
Of days filed with clouds.
Of minutes having strain.
Life on earth not easy.
Seconds spent in vain.
Trying to discover.
The direction of the train.
Of our lives trajectory
Without becoming insane,
And losing our lives because
We can't understand the rain.
That has suddenly appeared.
Most often this is the norm.
The state of our journey.
The appearance of a storm.
On this soil below.
A big old ball of dirt.
Where we live out our show.
Where we can be hurt.
On a stage often neglected.
By others we try to impress..
Yet sometimes we fall down
And make our lives a mess.
Because the struggle is real.

And sometimes we can't pretend.
All is well in our world.
The truth no longer we can bend.
We don't feel like smiling.
It hurts our face so much.
A frown is so much easier.
To put on for a bunch
Of hours when our forehead
Is furrowed deep in thought.
About the wrong we chose
And how our lives are fraught.
With perils and missteps.
We took the wrong path.
But let me entertain you
With a good belly laugh.
The joke we call life.
Is part of a master plan.
And if we choose the light.
Better days are in demand.
Yes gracious weeks are ahead.
Explore the best options.
The narrow lane instead
Of the wide road
That leads to destruction.
Live your life on purpose.
And watch how you'll function.
At a much higher level.
Just around the junction.
The best is yet to come.
And yes your heavenly Maker
He'll let you have some fun.
Be you a cook or a baker.
He'll guide you into.
A better way to be.
And live out your days.
In a place truly free.

Dripping Heart

You Have To Reach The Mountain

You have to reach the mountain,
You must climb to the top.
You can't get weary,
You cannot stop.
Until you reach your goal
The road you must travel.
To fulfill your soul
You can't unravel.
You mustn't falter
Trudge on ahead.
Take each stride
Tread by tread.
Cause it's little by little
The steps you take.
It's bit by bit
So stay awake.
And never slumber
On your path.
Life is long
And you must last.
You must go forward
Day by day.
No matter how trying
Your course to stay
So continue onward
Climb up the steps.
Only you can do it
For your own health.
For the peace of mind
You will find.
The path to your journey
And to divine.
The road only

Meant just for you.
Only you can do it
To yourself be true.
Complete your mission
It must be done.
Before you can sing
About how you have won.

Did you Ever Feel Like That?

Did you ever feel like that?
Just what am I saying?
Did you ever feel you could
Perform without portraying?
Who you really are
Up upon the stage,
Of your life expressly
When you came of age.
Did you ever desire to be
Someone you are not?
Did you ever want to feel
The cold and not the hot?
Did you ever want to elevate
Your game to another level?
Did you ever stop to think
Maybe you are, a daredevil?
And perhaps you are adventurous
Even though you haven't tried,
To show others that side of yourself
It's all tucked away inside.
Did you ever try to free yourself
To be all you can be?
Did you ever recognize who you are
One of high pedigree?
Able to leap tall buildings
And fly around in space.
Put on a Superman suit
A big smile on your face.
You may not have thought
You have super powers.
You only knew you could withstand
The rain and the showers,
That came into your life

That's how it always goes.
You must accept the sunny days
Along with the snows,
That come and make mountains
Of snowdrifts you can climb.
Did you ever realize
Snow melts and you'll be fine?
Getting back to the narrative
That's all I have to say.
Stop and think of who you are
On any given day.

Old Age

Old age.
This is the time.
We're out our prime.
And we feel life has passed us by.
We try and put back the pieces
Of the reese's peanut butter cups
And the love we once shared
With someone who was always there,
But now gone.
Our phone seldom rings,
The kids all big and the things
They do are technologically new to us.
We trust in an uncertain future.
As our friends pass.
Life doesn't last.
And we go to the gym
To get back some vim
And vigor.
The rigors
Of this time
Our bodies no longer
Towing the line.
But mysterious aches and ailments.
Suddenly appear.
As we face the fear
Of death.
Where will the wealth
Of our knowledge go?
Will we end the show
Of our lives
With a whimper or a banggggggggggggggggggggggggggg?
Or can we hang in there
A little bit longer?

And become stronger
Leaving a legacy.
For the descendants to see
How they can be
Living their lives more
Prosperously.

Struggle

The ruthlessness of life
Where all isn't fair.
When you try to take a bite
Of the pie in the air.
When you push against
The goads on the side.
You perform in the circus
Front and center ringside.
You feel like a clown
Big nose and all
Then your face wears a frown
Not really having a ball.
When you cross the river
The tide is rising high
When you start to shiver
After falling in the brine.
When you try to stay
Afloat by any means.
When the waves do play
And you don't feel so keen.
Then a whale swallows you up
So distressed you feel inside.
Volcanoes begin to erupt
So you want to run and hide.
When the earth won't yield
The seeds that you planted.
You are left far afield.
Your vision getting slanted.
And the Dow goes down and down
NASDAQ, ditto to that.
And your money can't be found
Your wallet, not looking so fat.
And life starts to look like

Groundhog day all over again.
And the one you loved
No longer is your friend.
So you begin to think
The universe is not very nice.
Putting you on the brink
Of jumping into arctic ice.
But think twice
Just do what you need
To preserve your life.
It will all be
Totally, alright.

I Never Seem To Have Enough Time

I never seem to have enough time.
Hours always slip away.
When I start something today
The time begins to say.
Hurry and finish your project
Cause you know minutes are fleet.
Do it fast and remember
You only have 7 days in a week.
Whenever I try to slow down
Because work demands precision.
It's when all the claims
On my time start on a collision.
Seconds crash into minutes
And minutes into hours, true.
What I think takes a short while
Ends up lasting more than I knew.
I want to make a request.
I want to ask the skies.
Can I have a little more time
Than all the girls and guys?
That live on planet earth.
Spinning around the sun.
I'm not really from here.
I'm just here to have fun.
But time on my planet,
Is different than on earth, see.
Where I'm from time dispenses
In a separate type of degree.
One minute in this world
Is only 1 second on mine.
So all you have to do
Is addition and multiply
The days and weeks and hours.

Add up to much more I guarantee.
So when I am at home
I have plenty of time for me.
But when I am right here
In this land where others dwell.
The duration of things occurring
Has put me under it's spell.
Cause I'm so constrained
Like in prison all locked up.
Not enough days to exist happily
Not enough moments in my cup.

Unchained

Unchained
Unchained and unleashed,
Let out the beast.
Be who you really are.
Be your own superstar.
Be the one who lives.
Inside where you can give,
Yourself a chance to grow.
And get on with your own show.
You're the best in this hour.
Only you have the power.
Only you can make the choice
To hear your own voice.
Which tells you how to be.
And what things you ought to see.
And how your life should flow.
Know, the way you should glow.

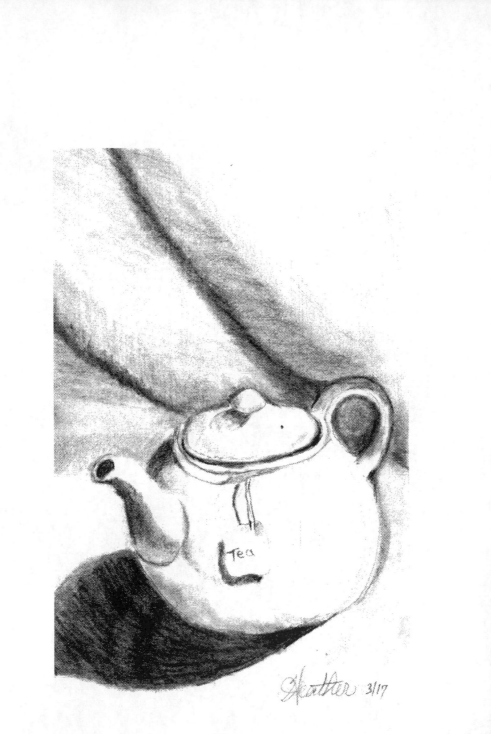

Teapot

Magnificence

There's a magnificence
In the moment.
There's a madness
At this hour.
There's a struggle
In the heavens.
There's a rain
That begins to shower.
There's a lightness
In this season.
There's a song
To be sung.
There's a movement
To discover.
There's a reason
The war was won.
There's a life
That has to be.
Lived all
On it's own.
There's a distance
You must travel.
There's a way
To get back home.
There's a notion
I once had.
An idea inside
My head.
Of how
My life can be.
When my heart
Takes flight instead.

Sometimes When You Talk

Sometimes when you talk to yourself,
You get your own answers.
Sometimes when you muse alone,
Thoughts begin to transfer.
From your mind to your heart
Or from the heart up to your mind.
You'll find out what you need to know,
And where you need to climb.
Which road to take
And which one to avoid.
The path well trodden
Or the one mostly devoid.
From the eyes of searchers who
Need to seek a way.
To live their lives in a
Most conspicuous way.
To be vocal or largely silent.
To talk or to shut up.
Sometimes we want to say things.
And sometimes not so much.
To be quiet at certain times.
I think is a very good thing
To treasure peace in your heart.
And the joy it brings,
To your spirit when you
Do your meditations alone.
Start your yoga in the morning
And don't pick up the phone.
To see who texted and who did not.
You really don't need to know.
Quiet times restores your soul.
And settles all your mind just so.
It helps you choose the path for you.

One on which you want to find.
All your life and what to do
With all your valued time.
Making your life so precious
Making your days sublime.

Why?

Why?
Is the question of the hour.
Sometimes it rains and showers.
And clouds fill the sky.
And troubles come nearby.
And you question in your mind.
And answers you seek to find.
The main one being this.
Why can't I get my wish.
When I want something to be.
It runs and starts to flee
The very thing I want.
I can't have that jaunt.
The very thing I have.
I want to let go bad.
I'm always thinking ahead.
And jumping on the sled.
Carrying me into the future.
Where life I imagine is cuter.
Than where I'm at today.
This time here has no sway.
But life goes on anyway.
Paying me no attention today.
So it is I who must,
Learn how to adjust.
To what's happening now.
And live today somehow.
With what's on my plate.
Instead of twisting fate.
And running thru future's gate.
I must lean to wait.
And live this now time
Knowing this present is sublime.

My Heart Is Filled With Laughter

My heart is filled with laughter.
My heart is filled with glee.
I have to wonder after
Will I be so free?
My heart is flying upward.
My heart's travelin' I agree.
Just what makes me smile,
What puts me on my knees?
To say a prayer of thanks.
To say and to believe.
Laughter, the best medicine.
Laughter is all you need.
To make your day go better
By degree to degree.
Break out into a chuckle.
Let joy make you breathe.
Sometimes you hold your breath.
Just because you're stressed.
Let out a big guffaw.
Let tension leave your nest.
And seek to see your cheeks.
Crunch closer to your ears.
It will make you happy.
And dissolve all your fears.

Some People Got The Vision

Some people got the vision.
Some people got the sight.
Some people can hear.
Mysteries day and night.
Some people look beyond.
Into another realm.
Some people take the wheel.
Of a different helm.
Some people listen good.
Some people are able to
Discern different secrets.
It's all that they can do.
To blot out the noise
Of this very earth.
And to tune into
Things that have more worth.
Than all the noise and chatter
Around us every day.
To hear the heavenly voices,
To hear what they say.
That you are a mighty being,
Your strength is in your core.
From your very heart.
Just open up the door.
Go inside and listen.
Quiet things around
Into your very center,
Your truth can be found.
So shut the door and listen.
And hear the celestial song.
Know your God is speaking.
His voice can be found.
Seek His higher wisdom.

Know He waits beside.
Then you will be able.
To live in Him and abide.
With peace in your spirit
With joy in your heart.
He's the only one
Who from you won't depart.
You'll never be alone.
He's there beside you now.
Be glad and very happy.
To Him make your bow.

I'm Spreading Out

I'm spreading out,
To the left and the right.
The sky is open
Birds taking flight.
The earth is amazing.
Filled with animals and such.
The feel of a mother
Giving baby a touch.
Of love that waits
For all of time.
A mother's love
Will always shine.
Life is expressive
See how it flows.
The river is wide
And knows where to go.
Time marches on
The sunset of my years.
Began with a cry
As a child with it's tears.
But now the curtain closes.
Did I read my lines well?
Only my children
Will be able to tell.
If I lived my life
To be the very best.
Before I sleep
And take my rest.

Hand holding trees and mountain

I Was Here On Earth

I was here on earth for a minute.
Even though the days seemed so long.
But when it's measured against eternity.
Those days were just a song.
A very small portion of time.
Hours passed so swift.
Started as a baby.
As a child we did lift,
Our own selves up.
We grew like Topsy did.
We realized as an adult.
We were no longer a kid.
Then shadowy days came.
But also sunlight too.
So the sun does arise.
Amidst the morning dew.
So love did blossom.
And then it wilted.
We had a lover.
We were maybe jilted.
But the earth kept on spinning.
Season after season.
Love was the purpose.
Love was the reason.

I Never

I never walk in a straight line,
I always go zigzag.
I never pick up the phone.
My tail I never wag.
I never listen to the king,
The queen has all the answers.
I don't believe in sickness,
I don't believe in cancer.
I never think inside the box,
I must step outside.
To me square pegs fit the locks
In round circles they do abide.
I always go the wrong way,
On streets that only show.
They are all one way
It's the other way I go.
But I do stop at red lights,
And pause at stop signs.
And I always obey
The intergalactic rhymes.
Coming from the heavens today,
When light comes thru the clouds.
Shining in the morning doesn't delay
Me shouting at sunbeams out loud.
I experience the life I've been given.
And I share a little bit,
Of the dreams I've hidden
Inside my memory kit.
Where all good things provide
A vision of the future.
Where all the fairies come and play
On wet forest moss that suits ya.
Inside the vastness of the woods

Full of birds and bumblebees.
I dance with the ugly trolls,
And I walk thru fallen leaves.
I prance around with Bambi,
And gentle wooded creatures.
It is the place I sometimes call
My home with glen like features.
And then I go back where,
I really do come from.
A far distant galaxy
Around the moon I roam.

You Are An Inspiration

You are an inspiration.
A true revelation,
Of light which finds itself
No longer on the shelf.
So long, I've longed
For a touch
From a much needed one.
Not much fun in my life
But somehow,
The shade draws down.
Clowns jump around.
And the poison pill
I swallowed
Hasn't kicked in yet.
You bet, I'm alive.
Not lost in a beehive
But jiving to the music
Of the beat.
And I repeat
The sweet sound
Of a profound one.
Not drowned
But swimming on the surface.
No longer cursed
But a phoenix rising.
As I try out new
Realities of personalities,
Hidden below my surface.
My face grinning now.
And from now on
I will pass go.
I will collect $ 200.00 dollars.

Count The Gray Hairs

Count the gray hairs on your head
Is it really bad?
Are there so many
That you don't have any
Or enough time
To do so?
Oh no!!!!!
Our flow maybe now
A little slower.
Takes longer to recover
From aches and pains.
The strains of past years
Evident thru old tears
And the wrinkle lines
In our eye corners.
Warn us of a stop light ahead
One day we'll be dead.
But let's not get morbid.
I just did a yoga pose
And almost froze
Into that position.
Like momma said
Don't leave that frown
On your face.
It'll stay in place, forever.
If you are truly clever
You will remember,
How you survived the ups
And downs of work.
And you raised a family.
You discovered a new path,
At this stage of you life.
You laugh at days to come.

And the setting sun
Of your years brings no more fear.
But cherished memories
Of past days lift the haze.
And you have no trepidation
Of the next life.
Just quiet and peace to come.
No more on the run.

What If I Were To Die

What if I were to die
Before the end of the day?
What if I passed by
And went far away?
What if I departed
No more with words to say?
What if I tried
To hide beyond the bay?
What if I wanted
To continue on the earth?
What if I told death
He has to reverse
His decision on my demise
And let me live longer still.
And to walk again
My days, to fulfill.
What if I let him know
I'm not going up in the clouds.
I am needed down here
To make my children proud.
I am needed to teach
The children all I know.
To let them access me
So that they can also grow.
I want to leave my legacy
For them to remember me by.
I want them to realize
Life is what you try.
And it is what you do
To the best of your ability.
In that you cannot lose

But only prosper happily.
When you've given your all
You will leave the best behind.
Before that final call
And before the tape unwinds.

Point And Counterpoint

Point and counterpoint.
Opposites attract.
The beginning and the ending.
Puts you on the map.
To find a balance.
Your life needs to know
Can you choose the right thing?
Can you find your flow?
Of how you want to do
A new thing in the earth
Of what you want to commit to.
Does it have value or any worth?
Does it help someone?
Does it make them find their way?
Does it gladden your heart?
To help them find their sway?
Does it point them to
A different way to play?
Out their days here
On this worldly clay.
Does it enlighten others
To seek the higher plain?
Does it help them to
Stand tall thru the rain
And strain that is life?
Does it help them
Hear the call?
Of the Masters message.
Does it help them to recall?
That through all the days.
The good and the bad.

That the Master was always there.
Through the happy and the sad.
And that He carried them.
When they couldn't see at all.
The way that they should choose.
The way to carry the ball.

Printed in the United States
By Bookmasters